Weather

Sally Morgan

Cherrytree Books are distributed in the United States
by Black Rabbit Books, P.O. Box 3263, Mankato, MN 56002

Printed in China.

Library of Congress Cataloging-in-Publication Data

Morgan, Sally.
  Weather / Sally Morgan.
     p. cm. -- (Helping our planet)
  Includes index.
  ISBN 978-1-84234-609-9 (library bound)
  1. Weather--Juvenile literature. I. Title. II. Series.

  QC981.3.M67 2011
  551.6--dc22

                        2010000383

First Edition
9 8 7 6 5 4 3 2 1

First published in 2009 by Evans Brothers Ltd.
2A Portman Mansions, Chiltern Street, London W1U 6NR, United Kingdom

Picture Credits:
Cover: main image Reinhard Dirscherl; inset, left to right: Robert Pickett, Robert Baldwin, Brian
Cushing; title page Michael Gore; p6 Fritz Polking; p7 Phillip Colla; p8 Robert Pickett; p9 Fritz Polking;
p10 Erik Schaffer; p11 Fritz Polking; p12 Peter Cairns; p13 Ian Harwood; p14 Reinhard Dirscherl; p15
Luc Hosten; p16 Robert Baldwin; p17 Quentin Bates; p18 Michael Gore; p19 Mike Whittle; p20 Stephen
Coyne; p21 Wayne Lawler; p22 Michael Gore; p23 Satyendra Tiwari; p24 Mike Maidment; p25 Brian
Cushing; p26 Robert Pickett; p27 Reinhard Dirscherl

Printed on chlorine free paper from sustainably managed sources.

Contents

Weather and Climate

What is the weather like where you are today?
Is it sunny or rainy, cold or hot? Weather changes
from day to day and from season to season. When
we talk about weather we are describing the
conditions that exist at the time.

▼ A rainy day did not stop this person
from taking a walk in the countryside.

Few people live in hot deserts. Instead, they choose places where they can farm the land and where there is a supply of water.

Climate is the regular pattern of weather over a year. Climate is important. It controls where people can live, and which crops farmers can grow. Most people live in areas where the climate is neither too hot nor too cold.

Find Out More

Use the Internet to find out about the climate of the place where you live. See if you can discover how the temperature and rainfall vary through the year.

Food and Climate

Crops depend on the climate. Different crops need different climates to grow well. We can only grow some crops, such as sugarcane, in places where it is hot all year round. We can grow other crops, such as potatoes, in a wide range of places.

▼ Wheat needs warm summers but does not grow well if the climate is too hot and dry.

You Choose

If you could live anywhere, where would you choose to live? Would you choose a place that was hot all year round or would you prefer a place that had seasons?

Rice needs a climate that is warm and wet.

Sometimes the climate is too cold for farmers to grow the crops people want to eat. So people bring in the foods from other parts of the world. For example, in northern Europe it is too cold for farmers to grow salad vegetables in winter. Instead, people bring them in from southern Europe where the climate is warmer.

Changing Climate

Twenty thousand years ago the Earth looked very different. A huge sheet of ice extended from the poles, and Europe and North America were freezing. Then the planet grew warmer and the ice melted.

The world's climates have been roughly the same for about 4,000 years, although there have been a few changes. For example, Europe had a Little Ice Age when some winters were so cold that rivers froze.

The glacier at the top of this mountain once reached all the way down the mountainside to the trees at the bottom.

Find Out More

During the coldest winters in Britain the River Thames froze over for months and people held fairs on the ice. Find out more about these fairs by visiting http://www.icons.org.uk/theicons/collection/the-thames/features/frost-fairs.

Now the climate is changing again. It is getting warmer. This is called global warming. The change is caused by an increase in gases such as carbon dioxide in the atmosphere.

▼ Power stations produce carbon dioxide when they burn oil, gas, or coal.

Keeping Us Warm

The Earth is surrounded by an atmosphere made up of different gases. These gases include nitrogen, oxygen, and carbon dioxide. Carbon dioxide is a gas that helps to keep the planet warm. It is called a greenhouse gas. Without the greenhouse gases the planet would be very cold and life would not survive.

▼ Glass traps heat inside this greenhouse, just like the greenhouse gases trap heat in the atmosphere.

Find Out More

Plants use carbon dioxide to make their own food. You can find out more about this at http://www.biology4kids.com/filesplants_photosyhthesis.html.

Now the amount of carbon dioxide and other gases in the atmosphere is increasing due to the activities of people. As a result, our planet is heating up.

▼ Rotting waste gives off methane, another of the greenhouse gases.

Fossil Fuels

Coal, gas, and oil are called fossil fuels. They are made from the remains of living organisms that died millions of years ago. Coal is made from trees and other plants while oil and gas are made from sea creatures.

▼ In this coal mine, people dig coal from the ground.

Fossil fuels contain carbon. When they burn in air, carbon dioxide is released. As people burn more fossil fuels, more carbon dioxide is released. This means that more heat is trapped in the atmosphere which warms up the surface of the planet.

What Can Be Done?

We need to reduce our use of fossil fuels. Some people are using wastes such as garbage and animal dung as fuels. The wastes produce a gas called biogas that people use for cooking, heating, and transportation.

This train in Sweden runs on biogas.

Rising Sea Levels

As the world gets warmer, the temperature of the oceans is rising. When water heats up, it expands and takes up more space. As a result, around the world sea levels are rising.

There is a lot of ice on planet Earth. It forms glaciers and the huge ice sheets at the North and South poles. Only a tiny rise in temperature is needed to make some of this ice melt.

The lives of arctic animals, such as these walruses, are put at risk by global warming.

This island in the Maldives could disappear underwater if sea levels rise. People have built stone walls to protect the land.

When the sea levels rise, low-lying land along the coast is flooded. In future low-lying coasts and islands may disappear under the sea.

What Can Be Done?

As the sea levels rise, threatened coastlines and islands can be protected. New sea walls can be built to protect the low-lying land.

Extreme Weather

Scientists think that as the oceans get warmer, there will be changes in the climate. There may be more violent storms called hurricanes.

Find Out More

In recent years, there have been some strong hurricanes in the Atlantic Ocean. Find out more about Hurricane Katrina that hit New Orleans in 2005. Go to http://www.timeforkids.com/TFK/katrina.

Heavy rains have flooded this city in Bangladesh.

Heatwaves and droughts may become common too. Temperatures may rise above normal and stay high for several weeks. Rain may fall mostly in the winter months, with little falling in summer.

▼ Parts of Africa, such as Ethiopia, have a dry climate. If the rains fail, crops die and people suffer from starvation.

Using Less Fuel

Much of the carbon dioxide that enters the atmosphere comes from burning fossil fuels. These fuels are used in power stations to make electricity and in the engines of cars, planes, and ships.

People can reduce the amount of fossil fuels burned each year by using less electricity or by using other energy sources such as sunlight and wind.

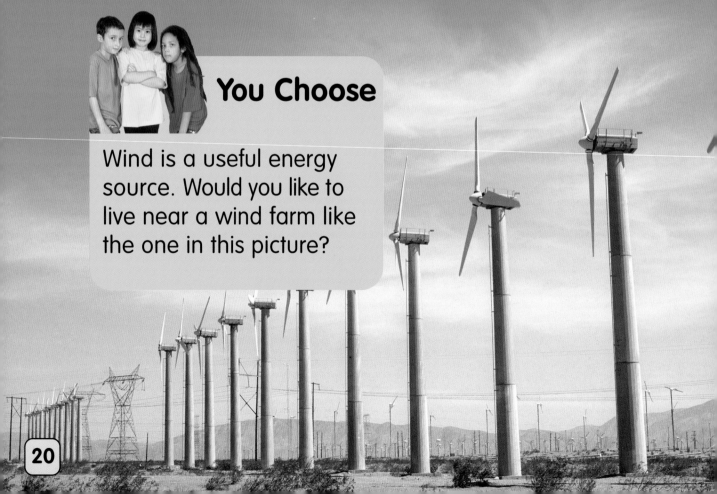

You Choose

Wind is a useful energy source. Would you like to live near a wind farm like the one in this picture?

We can reduce the amount of oil used for transportation too. People can make fewer trips, especially those by plane. Cars can be built to travel farther for each gallon of fuel they use. Also people can choose to walk, bike, or travel by public transportation such as buses and trains, rather than take the car.

The city of Vienna in Austria has a good public transportation system. Many people there travel on buses and trolleys.

Save the Forests

Trees are important as they take carbon dioxide from the air. But over the last 50 years, many of the world's forests, especially rain forests, have been felled or burned.

▼ People have planted trees outside this coal burning power station. The trees will take up some of the carbon dioxide that the power station produces.

We can protect the remaining forests and plant new ones. Trees such as willow grow very fast. We can cut the trees each year and use them for fuel.

What Can Be Done?

You can plant a tree! Often local conservation groups organize tree-planting days when volunteers plant hundreds of new trees.

See if you can plant some trees at your school, as these children are doing.

Effects On Animals

Climate change affects animals too. As the climate gets warmer, their habitats change. Warmer weather and droughts may cause plants to die, leaving animals with no food. Fires may destroy forests.

In the Arctic, the sea ice is melting earlier each year, threatening polar bears and other arctic animals.

However, some animals prefer a warmer world.
Butterflies are moving into areas where the winters
are getting warmer and there are fewer frosts.

The comma is a type of butterfly
that is gaining from global
warming. It is spreading north
where the winters are getting
milder. The butterfly can survive
well in these warmer winter
temperatures.

Find Out More

Use the Internet to find out more about climate change, how it
affects us and what we can do about it. Go to
http://epa.gov/climatechange/index.html.

Living With Change

Climate change is happening now, but there are things we can do to lessen the changes it brings. However, people will have to get used to living in a warmer world.

We can save water by collecting rainfall and using it to water plants.

We can design new homes to cope with extremes of weather. New homes may even have their own solar panels to trap energy from the sun and wind turbines to generate electricity. What would you like your future home to look like?

What Can Be Done?

It's important that we all save energy whenever we can. We can switch off lights when we leave a room and avoid leaving televisions and computers on standby.

his house has a grass roof nd large glass windows to ap heat.

Glossary

atmosphere the layer of gases around the planet

carbon dioxide one of the gases in Earth's atmosphere

climate the pattern of weather of a particular place

drought a long time without any rain

fossil fuels coal, gas or oil, fuels that are formed from the remains of living plants and animals

glacier a river of ice

global warming heating up of the planet

greenhouse gas a gas that traps heat in the atmosphere, such as carbon dioxide and methane

habitat the place where an animal or a plant lives

hurricanes violent storms that cause damage to large areas and threaten the lives of people and animals

rainforest a dense forest found in the hot and wet parts of the world

season one of four parts of the year — spring, summer, fall, and winter

solar panels panels that collect energy from the sun and turn it into energy we can use to light and heat our homes

starvation dying because of a lack of food

volunteers people who offer their help for free and do not get paid

wind farm a collection of wind turbines, machines that turn energy from the wind into electricity

Index

Numbers in **bold** refer to pictures.